Marsilius Graf von Ingelheim

The Design Process in Information System Research

Tasks and Challenges of a Science Discipline

Dokument Nr. V125917 aus dem GRIN Verlagsprogramm

Marsilius Graf von Ingelheim

The Design Process in Information System Research

Tasks and Challenges of a Science Discipline

GRIN Verlag

Bibliografische Information der Deutschen Nationalbibliothek: Die Deutsche Bibliothek verzeichnet diese Publikation in der Deutschen Nationalbibliografie; detaillierte bibliografische Daten sind im Internet über http://dnb.d-nb.de/ abrufbar.

1. Auflage 2009
Copyright © 2009 GRIN Verlag
http://www.grin.com/
Druck und Bindung: Books on Demand GmbH, Norderstedt Germany
ISBN 978-3-640-31772-1

The Design Process in Information Systems Research – Tasks and Challenges of a Science Discipline

Bachelorarbeit

eingereicht bei

Lehrstuhl für Betriebswirtschaftslehre,
insb. E-Finance and Services Science
Fachbereich Wirtschaftswissenschaften

Johann Wolfgang Goethe-Universität
Frankfurt am Main

von
cand. rer. pol. Marsilius Graf von Ingelheim

Studienrichtung: Wirtschaftswissenschaften (Finance & Accounting)
7. Fachsemester

Table of Contents

Number of words in total: 14894

Figures

Tables

1   Introduction

1.1   Motivation and Research Questions

The Information Systems (IS) research discipline is undergoing a serious identity crisis, seeking its sphere of activity to be relevant in practice and rigorous in scientific considerations. One reason for this is the strengthening of the Design Science approach. This new discipline developed as a synergy from aspects of engineering, architecture, and industrial design and is employed in the design of IT artifacts and software systems. Design Science is becoming a powerful trend in IS research (Vahidov 2006). It gives the IS discipline a new and more detailed focal point as pertains to the application of software and IT artifact development which is growing in importance in IS research over the time (Weber 2003; Orlikowski and Iacono 2001; Cross 2001). IS practitioners ask for new and innovative design approaches, dealing with the evolving organizational and inter-organizational tasks. The way these tasks are executed, in close cooperation with the practical business world, seems to be insufficiently considered. The debate in IS research is carried out between traditional scientists and the knowledge-producing researchers/practitioners and *"it could be argued that research aimed at developing IT systems, at improving IT practice, has been more successful and important than traditional scientific attempts to understand it"* (March and Smith 1995, p. 252).

IS researchers are mainly focused on the behavioral impact of new IT solutions within a business unit. These concepts are needed to describe the relationship between the humans and the technology. However, this way of conducting research is descriptive and evaluative. Instead of telling "what is" or "what will be", Design Science is giving guidance as to "how to do" things (Walls et al. 1992). The importance of this new approach is given through the rapid development of business needs and the increased necessity to solve business problems through the implementation of IT solutions. The knowledge base for designing new solutions has not yet been fully developed. IT consultants borrow knowledge from reference disciplines and apply this knowledge to present problems. This way of providing solutions is not compatible with Design Science as an area of research. A relevant design approach needs to give new answers to phenomena thus far unsolved.

However, the IS discipline has not yet established a solid groundwork for Design Science within its discipline. The Design Scientist needs to develop his/her own routines and competencies in form of standards to establish a framework, which can serve boundaries of and describe the ties within their discipline.

A philosophical underpinning is required to align the researchers of Design Science to the same route. Design Science needs to be effective and efficient (Hevner et al. 2004) to deal with the tasks that lie before it. Instead of applying available knowledge, Design Science has to establish itself as a pure research discipline (Weber 1987).

The IS discipline is an amalgamation of different and complex research areas that cannot be easily divided into single parts without losing their identities and the practical use of this discipline. However, scholars of the IS discipline are still in search for the core subject matter of IS research to be able to overcome the current identity crisis (e.g. Orlikowski and Iacono 2001; Alter 2003; Weber 2003).

The Design Scientists have developed various concepts and frameworks to describe the relevance of their discipline, which are described in the following chapters to give an insight in one of the research areas of IS research.

To develop this insight this paper investigates the following research questions:

1. Does the Design Science approach need to be linked to laws and areas of research of the Natural Sciences to be able to produce relevant outcomes?

This question is posed because a pure research discipline needs to develop clear boarders of the discipline. On the one hand this separation can be useful to focus on the core concept of Design Science, but on the other a separation can lead to irrelevant outcomes that lack realistic reference to the organizational contexts.

2. What should be regarded as the core subject matter of the Design Science discipline and why?

The core subject matter defines of each scientific discipline. The design approach risks focusing too much on a single element within the IS research cycle. Without incorporating various objects and possible questions, an IT artifact is unable to solve a class of problems. The core subject matter is needed as fixture with which to adjust the discipline. However, Design Science has not yet defined its core subject matter. Different approaches need to be analyzed.

3. Do current approaches to developing important Design Science frameworks focus on a core subject matter?

Finally this paper analyzes which core subject matter has been applied in the academic papers most often cited in Design Science history and how the discipline could possibly develop in the future.

1.2   Structure

This paper gives insight into the development of Design Science – one special part of IS research that has gained a lot of relevance within the last decades (e.g. Hevner et al. 2004; Walls et al. 1992, March and Smith 1995).

Chapter 2 highlights the relationship between Design Science and the Natural Sciences by regarding the historical development of design from one of the earliest Design Science definitions presented in 'The Sciences of the Artificial' (Simon 1996) through to the use of design in the IS world today. The chapter attempts to answer the question whether the Natural Sciences and Design Science can be regarded separately or only in combination within IS research? In closing Chapter 2 briefly examines the different philosophical approaches of Design Science and incorporates the question if Design Science is a paradigm itself.

Chapter 3 addresses the different Design Science concepts in academic IS literature. The considered frameworks construct different Design Science concepts that are interdependent in their combined view of design in IS research. The focus of this chapter lies on the use of design to create efficient and effective IT artifacts (Hevner 2004). The question is posed as to whether suggested frameworks see Design Science in IS as a separate and pure area of research. The role of the laws and approaches of the Natural Sciences in Design Science are also explored. The conclusion of this chapter presents different views of Design Science are have been offered by other scholars to give a more complete picture of the existing academic literature.

Chapter 4 examines the essential role of the core subject matter of the Design Science discipline in its defining and overcoming its identity crisis. The question is posed whether the IT artifact should be regarded as the basic research area in Design Science. The mostly cited academic articles in this area give an understanding of the possible use of the IT artifact within their frameworks. It is shown how the frameworks introduced in chapter 3 treat the IT artifact in their research projects. To give a brief contrast the idea of the Work System as core subject matter of Design Science is demonstrated in this chapter accompanied with the criticism of this approach.

Chapter 5 gives a conclusion of the paper and an outlook of a possible progress of Design Science in IS research.

2   Theoretical Background of Design Science

This chapter gives a brief introduction of the theoretical background of Design Science. The basic concept of design that emerged over time is described in section 2.1. This chapter gives also an insight into the common use of design and Design Science in the IS research discipline. Section 2.2 questions whether Design Science and Natural Science need to be connected or separated in order to pursue their aims of producing new knowledge and/or describing knowledge. The background for finding an appropriate answer of this question is deciding whether, and if so, under which conditions design can be regarded as a unique science discipline. The chapter compares the requirements of a science discipline with the characteristics of Design Science. This chapter focuses on the role of theory and theorizing in Design Science. Section 2.3 contrasts the different approaches of philosophical paradigms that can describe Design Science and poses the questions as to whether Design Science is a paradigm itself.

2.1   Introducing the Design Concept

Design is the process of changing present situations into preferred ones. Design creates something new that does not yet exist in nature and for this reason design is not comparable to the Natural Sciences that describe the objects and phenomena of the natural world (Simon 1969; Vaishna and Kuechler 2004). The study of designing things has long been a fundamental part of art, engineering, architecture and other disciplines in the business and industrial sectors. Design plays a key role in these areas by distinguishing the practical and professional side from the sciences of this particular discipline (Simon 1969). Only the artificial processes and products in the form of newly arranged artifacts can achieve the desired outcome in the practical world.

One major task in the development of the design field was the construction of a joint view of design and science to establish a theoretical foundation for design practices. The idea of design using parts of the traditional science disciplines has continuously emerged during the early decades of the 20th century. This resulted in the use of design based on scientific knowledge in industrial sectors, i.e. the so called "scientific design". It was not yet a synonym for Design Science but already an application of modern design practice (Cross 2001).

One highlight of this new way considering design was the book "The Sciences of the Artificial" by Herbert Simon published in 1969 (Simon 1969). Simon was one of the first to give the "Science of Design" a basis and definition, which will be considered at a later stage in this paper.

Some authors distinguish between two ways of looking at design in a scientific context by describing "Science of Design" as the study and the understanding of design and "Design Science" as a systematic approach to design that leads to a scientific design activity itself (Cross 2001). This might be important when arguing that the act of designing can never be a scientific activity itself in contrast to the study of design that can be subject of scientific investigation (Grant 1979).

In this paper the expressions "Design Science" and "Science of Design" will be used synonymously due to the fact that the important academic articles use Design Science in a scientific way without varying in their view of design as a scientific discipline (e.g. Hevner et al. 2004; Nunamaker et al. 1991; Walls et al. 1992). The idea of Design Science as a scientific activity will be further developed in this paper.

The IS discipline is strongly interrelated to design and Design Science due to its historical origins with a key focus on information and communication technology in organizational settings (Kuechler et al. 2007). The IS discipline is confronted with special requirements of the professional and practical business areas and must align these requirements in connection with the aspects of Behavioral Science that characterize the internal organizational structures.

Technology is practical and useful, therefore, IS practitioners and IS users are involved in design to improve the effectiveness and efficiency of their organization (March and Smith 1996; Walls et al. 1992; Hevner et al. 2004). However, the IS discipline uses various methodologies in a complex setting. Design Science displays the prescriptive component that can improve, for example, IT performance as a knowledge-using activity (March and Smith 1995). In the Computer Science discipline every machine is recognized as an artifact that has been designed to describe an experiment. Experiments can produce new knowledge by demonstrating the possible implementation of designed artifacts into the real world. This all is realized by using Design Science (Newell and Simon 1976).

This shows that Design Science is primarily a problem-solving domain leading to an innovative way of implementing and managing IS efficiently (Hevner et al. 2004). Benbasat and Zmud (1999) show that this problem-solving criterion is one of the core tasks of IS. They argue that an information system is irrelevant unless IS professionals can use its knowledge and to create practical value through implementation. The challenges for Design Science in information systems grows, as on the one hand IS professionals ask for further adaption of business and organizational knowledge into IT artifacts and on the other hand the needs and the expectations of newly designed knowledge for their business areas grows continuously.

2.2   Design Science as an Area of Research

The newly emerged Design Science discipline was developed on the basis of scientific knowledge that was used to develop innovative design products in an industrial context (Cross 2001). The available scientific knowledge was taken from the well-established Natural Sciences to substantiate the usefulness of the designed elements and to fill in for the missing theoretical foundation of designing elements. From this starting position from the "Scientific Design" the question is asked whether Design Science needs to be fully separated from the Natural Sciences in order to establish a strong and independent scientific discipline and whether an influential position of the Natural Sciences and their laws is essential to produce relevant new knowledge.

To give an answer to these important questions it is necessary to discuss the characteristics and the differences of Design Science and the Natural Sciences.

2.2.1 The Separation of Design Science and Natural Science

This section is addressing the first research question mentioned in the introduction. The characteristics of Design Science and Natural Sciences developed over time. This paper tries to find an answer and highlights already existing answers of whether both approaches need to be regarded separately or not.

It is a common opinion of IS scholars that the Natural Sciences are regarded as the descriptive way of looking at the world and its phenomena (e.g Hevner at al 2004; March and Smith 1995; Walls et al. 1992; Vahidov 2006). Assigned to the IT discipline the Natural Sciences form the understanding of the nature of IT. Although IT phenomena, mainly in the Computer Science discipline, are man-made and therefore not natural, the Natural Sciences can address these artificial phenomena by analyzing their "nature" of being (March and Smith 1995). This understanding consists of several approaches to produce scientific knowledge. Natural Science research methods are normally composed of a developmental part and a justifying part (Hevner et al. 2004). Through the developmental part, the scientists attempt to characterize naturally occurring phenomena with the help of special sets of concepts and ways of describing the natural reality (March and Smith 1995). This side of the Natural Sciences concludes with the formulation of scientific theories and the proposition of new natural laws. These theories and laws form an understanding of the explored phenomena, which is not yet fully described in the terms demanded by the Natural Sciences. The missing part is the explaining or justification part of analyzing phenomena (March and Smith 1995; Hevner et al. 2004). The testing of theory plays a key role in the Natural Sciences (Venable 2006) as only the tested, justified, and validated theory or law can be included into the knowledge base of the accordant discipline.

One discipline of the Natural Sciences that should be regarded in this context is the discipline of Behavioral Science. Behavioral Science should not be seen in contrast to the broader view of the Natural Sciences that include e.g. physics, biology, and the social sciences; in fact it is one of the specialized disciplines that is closely related to IS research. Simon (1969) argues that many disciplines tend to focus on Behavioral Science and not on Design Science, this is also true for IS research (Carlsson 2006). IS mainly deals with the interaction between people, technology, and organizations and attempts to describe their interdependencies (Hevner et al. 2004).

In contrast to the descriptive and explanatory character of Natural Science, the Design Science approach plays a prescriptive part of the scientific interest in IT (March and Smith 1995). Instead of trying to understand the existing phenomena with the use of scientific instruments, Design Science gives an answer to heretofore unsolved organizational problems. The design approach in the sense of IS research being aimed at broadening the possibilities for implementing of the use of IT in organizational contexts. It is therefore a problem-solving discipline (Simon 1969; Hevner et al. 2004).   Technical knowledge grows rapidly, and the need for IT solutions for new application areas grows continuously (Markus et al. 2002). Design Science gives an answer through developing knowledge that had been non-existent up to this point. This knowledge is not only represented in theories or the way defining it, it is also a process of developing innovative artifacts that comply with the ideas, practices, technical capabilities, and products that are needed for the special requirements of IS in form of analysis, design, and implementation (Hevner and March 2003). Design Science is *"a body of intellectually tough, analytic, partly formalizable, partly empirical, teachable doctrine about the design process"* (Simon 1969 p.113). In other words, the research in Design Science is the design process and the way of building a new artifact is similar to building a new theory in the Natural Sciences. One major task in the design process is the description of the desired organizational capabilities that need to be provided by the artifact. Without the identification of the organizational problem, the design process is not able to address it effectively (March and Storey 2008).

Beside this design process, Design Science always produces a physical artifact. This product is essential for the evaluation process that is necessary to give a proof of feasibility of the (theoretical) constructed artifact in its organizational context (Hevner et al. 2004). The implementation evaluates the effectiveness and efficiency of the artifact in its desired environment, as we need to recognize that the business organization, which forms the environment in most of the cases, is an artifact itself designed and constructed to achieve specific purposes of the business world (Srinivasan et al. 2005). Each organizational framework differs from each other with implications for the design process. It is not possible to set up a general law or theory that describes the operational sequences within a business unit. The hypotheses and desired specifications can be proven only by constructing the artifact (Walls et al. 1992). The designed artifact needs to be implemented to give a concrete assessment of the artifact's suitability to its intended purpose (Hevner and March 2003).

This necessity supports the idea of Design Science being an area of research with the characteristics "build" and "evaluate" (March and Smith 1995). Research is normally associated with the idea of generating knowledge that can be transferred to general settings (Gregg et al. 2001). The design process needs to demonstrate that no other already existing IT artifact is able to present a solution to the problem at hand. The new IT artifact should not be an adaption of existing knowledge into the design process; instead it has to be the development and creation of new knowledge that will be included into the knowledge base to demonstrate a research process in IS research. Scientific research is defined as the *"use of scientific knowledge directed toward the production of useful material, devices, systems, or methods, including design and development of prototypes and processes"* (Blake 1978 cited in Gregg et al. 2001).

The IT artifact can be subject of further evaluation to give a better understanding of the value the IT artifact has added to the knowledge base and to the organization. This way of evaluating should not be confused with the Natural Sciences activity of explaining how and why an artifact works (March and Storey 2008; March and Smith 1995).

Figure 1 shows how the knowledge base is connected with the design process (Owen 1997). The design process is given through the channel on the knowledge using side. Through a structured process (for example one of the Design Science frameworks that are introduced later in this paper) available IT knowledge is used to set up the basic model of each IT artifact. As we noticed before, the design process uses an immense amount of new knowledge that is produced within the design process; however, some basic ideas and structures are taken out of the existing knowledge base. The produced IT artifact can be seen as the "works" depicted in Figure 1. The artifact itself is a piece of knowledge, a proof of concept in the organizational framework (Hevner et al. 2004). The evaluation process of the innovative artifact within the Design Science discipline makes it possible to transfer the new knowledge back into the knowledge base through a structured channel defined by Design Science frameworks.

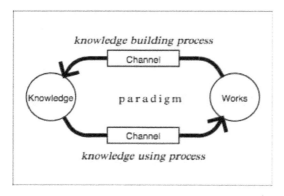

Figure 1: Knowledge Building and Knowledge Using Process (Owen 1997)

The channels on both sides can also be influenced by other disciplines. As we noted before, Behavioral Science aspects play a major role in the justification of Design Science in IS research. Without this context, Design Science is not able to produce artifacts that make business organizations more effective and efficient (Hevner and March 2003).

Simon (1969) describes the "artificial sciences" as constrained from two directions at simultaneously: (1) the outer environment and (2) the inner environment. The outer environment is given in form of parameters, in this case through the organizational composition in which the artifact has to operate. The other dimension is the inner environment, the organization of the artifact itself. *"The bringing-to-be of an artifact, components and their organization, which interfaces in a desired manner with its outer environment, is the design activity"* (Vaishna and Kuechler 2004 p. 2). This basic design definition makes clear that the design process is constrained through natural laws (i.e. technological, organizational, and behavioral) of its outer environment; therefore, it is necessary to understand these laws to create an artifact. However, occasionally the laws constraining the design results are not fully understood, this is the reason why implementations are necessary in order to gain insight into the laws affecting the possible reaction of the artifact in its provided environment (Srinivasan et al. 2005).

Each IT artifact contributes to the IT knowledge base and can be subject of the evaluation of Natural Science disciplines. Design Science informs e.g. the Behavioral Science discipline with its final act of implementing a new artifact in a business organization. The artifact becomes the focus of expanded and continuing research (Nunamaker et al. 1991). Behavioral Science is able to recognize why the artifact works and can challenge the design discipline to build more effective artifacts, this constitutes progress in IS research.

A possible answer to the posed research question is that the design process is able to create bridges between the human processes and the technological capabilities of IS research (Gregg et al. 2001). It is not useful to isolate both science approaches of Design Science and the Natural Sciences as otherwise the described bridge is not able to connect the strength of both disciplines. The outcomes of the joint view are able to solve relevant problems in the real business world without sacrificing the traditional science criteria. However, it is not possible to give a binding answer to this question as it is constrained by the focus point each scholar sets for his or her own research. This focus point is connected with the understanding of the core subject matter of IS research. This question will be analyzed in chapter 4.

To be able to install the obtained knowledge out of the design process into the knowledgebase, a theoretical foundation must be set up to provide a background for further scientific research in the analyzed area. The question needs to be answered whether Design Science must develop a strong theoretical foundation within the discipline itself or if the theoretical foundation laid by the Natural Sciences suffices.

2.2.2 Theorizing in Design Science

This section provides brief insight into the use of theory and theorizing in Design Science discipline. Several authors have addressed the role of theory in Design Science. Although some authors exclude theorizing from Design Science and regulating it rather to the Natural Sciences (e.g. March and Smith 1995, Hevner et al. 2004), this paper recognizes the importance of theory building in the design process. The possibilities of theorizing in Design Science discipline are highlighted to focus on an area that is part of the overall Design Science and IS research discussion. This focus also contributes to the demand of Design Science being an area of research because theory plays a key role in the traditional Natural Sciences. The use of theory helps to distinguish between research and other efforts such as consulting or programming (Gregg et al. 2001). However, this section seeks not to forestall special objectives of the Design Science frameworks covered in Chapter 3. Instead, general insight into the role of theory is the basis for this analysis.

This paper already discussed the physical artifact as the key element of each Design Science process. The prescriptive nature of Design Science pretends to give answers to real world phenomena and problems, posed mainly by the business world. Therefore, the necessary relevance is provided by the proof-of-demonstration through the implementation of IT artifacts that are designed to provide a solution for the stated problem. The artifact remains the most visible output of Design Science, but it is not necessarily the only output of Design Science research processes (Purao 2002).

Nunamaker et al. (1991) has already noted that Design Science (here: Systems Development) is in need for a multimethodological approach where the building of an artifact is only one part of the research cycle. Figure 2 demonstrates one possible conception of the outputs of Design Science described by Purao (2002). Beside the artifact as an output of the design process and as the commonly used design element in an organizational context, two other levels are introduced in this framework. The focus in this section lies on the dotted oval of Figure 2 that displays theory as a potential output of the Design Science process. Knowledge as operational principle is outside the scope of this discussion (not all three forms will be produced in every design process) (Purao 2002).

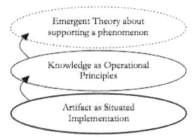

Figure 2: The Outputs of Design Research (Purao 2002)

In this context the role of theory is important to improve the relevance and utility of a designed artifact. Theory in Design Science firstly provides guidance for the scientist to find a way that is effective and feasible in carrying out a design process (Walls et al. 1992). The introduction of theory into the design process provides the necessary instructions for other researchers to identify the problem space. The theory prepares the knowledge for undertaking the building of an artifact in form of process knowledge and design principles (Gregor 2002). The researchers are able to test the produced artifact in similar problem situations and, therefore, make a contribution to the advanced knowledge base of the discipline (Venable 2006). This guidance in a generalized and abstracted way distinguishes the Design Science process from a specialized consulting project that deals only with an isolated phenomenon (Gregor 2002). The implemented artifact is not self-explanatory and the methodological construction of an artifact is the object of theorizing. The proof-of-demonstration that is provided by the implementation can be regarded as a proof of the underlying method (Vaishnavi and Kuechler 2005). Furthermore the theory can initially give a statement of relationships among constructs that can be tested (Gregor 2006). The interaction of the technological and the social systems that are part of the designed object demonstrates the most important connection that should be analyzed by an explanatory theory. Gregor (2006) characterizes this form of theory as a desirable end product that provides a clear view of the organizational consequences of IS research. Theories are the basis for identifying which classes of things can be realized through Design Science in the form of new ideas, concepts, and construction of frameworks. The artifact provides the link between technologically based theories and the organizational impact of the designed object; additionally a theory is needed to describe the multimethodological features of IS research in the form of nature, the social world, and artificial objects (Nunamaker et al. 1991; Gregor 2006).

The difference of design theory relative to traditional theory is the normative or prescriptive way of saying, "how something should be done" (Gregor 2002). This dimension of theory in IS research is given through the guidance for practitioners. Practitioners need to know how a specific technology is used to solve a particular phenomenon. This insight gives them the opportunity to identify the relevant technology out of the body of knowledge of the IS discipline to solve their real world problems in an efficient and effective way (Venable 2006).

This paper has noted that Design Science is in need of theory and theorizing within its discipline. The special role of theory in Design Science frameworks will be highlighted in Chapter 3.

To complete the theoretical background of Design Science, epistemological and ontological questions need to be posed. The next section tries to give an answer as to whether an already existing research paradigm can be used as the basis for Design Science, or whether Design Science needs to develop a paradigm itself.

2.3   Establishing a Philosophical Basis for Design Science

It is generally accepted by scholars of the field that the IS discipline is still in search of an own identity. This search process appears throughout various papers and various approaches suggested that attempt to establish a philosophical basis for IS research (e.g. McKay 2005; Weber 1987; Gregg et al. 2001). There has been a call for a paradigmatic concept that forms the foundation of each design process (Weber 1987). However, the most important question in this section is whether Design Science can incorporate itself into an existing paradigmatic framework or whether

Design Science needs to form a paradigm itself. To meet the concerns of the several authors, this section attempts to cover the different basic approaches that are used the most in the discussion.

In section 2.2.2 this paper recognized that the Design Science discipline provides guidance to researchers through the formulation of Design theories. The question of an epistemological (and ontological) background can help the researchers to find a collective way of constructing theories and providing guidelines for conducting IS research (Gregor 2006). The shared beliefs, concepts, and frameworks of a research discipline are normally based upon a paradigm that supports the communication within the discipline. Without a general basis given by a paradigm providing a framework, the research efforts cannot be based on a common foundation and each researcher must individually define his or her own Design Science procedures. This hinders progress in this discipline, and it is not possible for researchers to determine if a design process constitutes high quality research (Weber 1987; Gregg et al. 2001).

IS research traditionally follows from a Positivist or Interpretive approach (Gregg et al. 2001). This paper incorporates the Critical approach that is mentioned in Orlikowski and Baroudi (1991) as a background for the Socio-technologist paradigm that was developed into a finalized concept by Gregg et al. (2001). Table 1 outlines the major assumptions of the research paradigms treated by Gregg et al. (2001) in the form of ontology, epistemology, and methodology.

Basic beliefs	Positivist/ postpositivist	Interpretive/ constructivist	Socio-technologist/ developmentalist
Ontology • What is the nature of reality?	One reality; knowable with probability	Multiple socially constructed realities	Known context with multiple socially and technologically created realities
Epistemology • What is the nature of knowledge?	Objectivity is important; researcher manipulates and observes in dispassionate objective manner	Interactive link between researcher and participants; values are made explicit; created findings	Objective/Interactive; Researcher creates the context and incorporates values that are deemed important
Methodology • What is the approach for obtaining the desired knowledge and understanding?	Quantitative (primarily); interventionist; decontextualized	Qualitative (primarily); hermeneutical; dialectical; contextual factors are described	Developmental (primarily); focus on technological augmentations to social and individual factors

Table 1: Major Research Paradigms and the Characteristics of their Major Beliefs (Gregg et al. 2001)

Positivist Approach

The Positivist approach is the leading philosophical definition in today's IS research (Orlikowski and Baroudi 1991). This approach is primarily based on an empirical world-view seeking to obtain knowledge through quantitative methods. The reason for this methodological procedure is the notion that reality is existent only in one reality (Gregg et al. 2001). This reality is not disrupted by the action of humans, and social worlds are not influenced by the actions of their members. This reality consists of a social world that is controlled by nature and therefore can be regarded as analogous to the natural world. Table 1 describes this as "knowable with probability", thus, the reality can only be discovered without a direct impact. The research efforts are independent from the analyzed object; hence the researcher plays only a passive role and IS research for example is not able to change the social context (Orlikowski and Baroudi 1991).

Interpretive Approach

The supporters of the Interpretive approach see the world as a social process (Orlikowski ans Baroudi 1991). Social systems cannot be regarded independently and without the influence of their members. As Table 1 shows, individuals, organizations or groups individually construct the social systems because every user has special requirements that must be addressed by the system. These researchers seek to understand the social process. This explanation must then be interpreted. The methodologies used are mainly qualitative and in the form of field studies and the exposure of special sets of constructs to social effects (Gregg et al. 2001; Orlikowski and Baroudi 1991).

These research paradigms are able to embrace many research concepts of the IS research discipline. However, they are not able to cover Design Science completely, due to the normative and prescriptive nature of Design Science that asks, "how things should be".

Socio-technologist Approach and the Research Paradigm Concept

Weber (1987) calls for a paradigm that covers the design discipline completely and is not borrowed or composed out of another area of research. He argues that Design

Science shall not be established as a "pure" discipline unless it develops a paradigm of its own. Otherwise Design Science will be regarded as an "applied" discipline. This status is undesirable as the discipline would then not be able to produce its own right to exist due to the fact that the conducted research mainly contributes to the reference discipline that is grounded on the paradigm applied. Weber suggests that the Design Science discipline should develop a paradigm through the comparative advantages that this discipline can realize. Therefore, he draws upon the concept of the inner and outer environments first mentioned by Simon (1969). The comparative advantage of Design Science is seen to be the development of innovative artifacts described as the inner environment. The outer environment should not be part of the new paradigm as this is the concern of other disciplines. Weber argues that natural laws, which form the outer environment, are automatically effective for the artifact because the raw materials of the design process are objects constrained by natural laws.

Weber does not take into account the core of Design Science. Simon (1969) describes the design process as the space between the inner and outer environment. The change of present situations into preferred ones can be incorporated completely into a new system of "characteristics" and "behaviors". Therefore, it is not predetermined that the designed artifact shall act completely as the natural laws would force it to do. However, if this were to happen and natural laws could predict the characteristics and the behavior of the artifact within its provided organizational context, Design Science would loose its need and eligibility of implementing the artifact as a proof-of-demonstration. In this scenario the Natural and Behavioral Sciences would be able to predict the impact of an introduced artifact on a business unit without a need for information from the implementation process. Orlikowski and Baroudi (1991) share are a similar approach, when they say that IS research should not preclude the use of knowledge of other disciplines to the advantage of the individual research topic.

Nevertheless, Gregg et al. (2001) also recognizes the need for an individual Design Science paradigm to address the unique requirements of Design Science. However, another focus as proposed by Weber (1987).

Gregg et al. (2001) recommended introducing a third paradigm that exists in harmony with the Positivist and Interpretive approach already described before. As shown in Table 1, Gregg et al. (2001) introduce the Socio-technologist paradigm. This paradigm is to give an answer to the missing requirements of Design Science. First of all it should be clarified that the Socio-technologist paradigm is in many ways similar to the Critical paradigm (e.g. Orlikowski and Baroudi 1991). This paper adopts the denotation of Gregg et al. (2001) in recognition of the overall concept and the focus on Design Science presented by the authors.

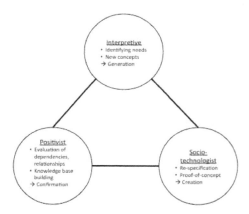

Figure 3: The Research Paradigm Concept (own Diagram following Gregg et al. (2001))

The Socio-technologist paradigm acknowledges the use of technology in the social world. Furthermore, the paradigm regards reality as technologically shaped. The individual elements of reality do not exist independently from each other. The context creates the realities as stated in Table 1 and this context can be influenced through design activities. Figure 3 points out the relationships between the three analyzed paradigms. It is significant that Gregg et al. (2001) have developed a framework related to the multimethodological approach to IS Research developed by Nunamaker et al. (1991).

Nunamaker et al. (1991) introduced

- Theory Building

- Experimentation

- Observation

- Systems Development

as elements of their framework. Gregg et al. (2001) see the starting point in identifying needs for the attracted phenomena. The social connections described in this paradigm are the basis for developing new concepts. The use of the Interpretive paradigm can be paralleled by the research strategy "Theory Building" in Nunamaker et al. (1991). Both conceptions introduce the methods and concepts used to solve a real world problem. Furthermore, it can be regarded as the problem space that is set up to develop the design process. However, the Interpretive paradigm is the starting point of each Design Science research effort with the keyword being "Generation" as defined by Gregg et al. (2001). The Positivist paradigm is able to evaluate the dependencies and relationships among the concepts and methods without the risk of implying an interpretation into the evaluation. This neutral and passive observation is the basis for an independent knowledge base that can be seen in conjunction with the Nunamaker et al. (1991) concept of "Observation" in combination with "Theory building". The Interpretive paradigm needs to be incorporated when an evaluation of the social behavioral is required. The "Experimentation" strategy is built in the Positivist view. This paradigm is abstracted with the word "Confirmation" that includes research strategies and research methodologies to confirm relationships when little is known about the underlying phenomenon (Nunamaker et al. 1991).

Finally, the new Socio-technologist paradigm is responsible for the development of an artifact that can be based on the "Generation" and "Confirmation" of the linked paradigms and is therefore abstracted to "Creation". If the system is not yet able to provide an answer for the posed phenomena, a re-specification and modification of the concepts and theories is necessary. Thus, the Socio-technologist paradigm is again strongly connected with the Interpretive and Positivist paradigms that adapt to changes (Gregg et al. 2001). In Nunamaker et al. (1991) the parallel strategy is "Systems Development". This strategy incorporates the necessary steps to build a working artifact. The artifact is seen as proof-of-concept in both frameworks that displays the success of the research process given in combination with the technology transfer to an organization. Hence, the evaluation process that is needed to round up the scientific research cycle is the final link between the three paradigms.

Nunamaker et al. (1991) state that *"it is extremely important that other research methodologies be employed to support systems development efforts because development of a software system by itself usually is not considered a serious IS research project"* (p.95).

Systems development is a subset and not completely the same process as Design Science (Venable 2006). As this paper noted before, Design Science regards software development as part of its discipline. The strong connection to Behavioral Science, the need of theory and theorizing, and the implementation of the designed artifact in an organizational context are examples that provide the necessary reasons as to why all of the mentioned paradigms are needed to cover the entire Design Science research process.

McKay (2005) argues that Design Science is not a paradigm itself, but a body of knowledge of the IS field. This paper follows McKay's conception because the analysis shows that the different research methods and the different perspectives derived from the three paradigms are essential to display a Design Science process that is rigorous in research, effective and efficient for users, and provides an object for further research in the different science disciplines.

It is understood that some authors attempt to define IT artifact more narrowly so as to promote an understanding of the design process seen as the inner environment of Design Science. However, this paper attempts to display Design Science as a discipline that is part of IS research. It uses the benefits from the Natural Science disciplines and considers the system development part (inner environment) as the major contribution to the design process – but inefficient and ineffective without the influences from the outer environment.

3   Developing the Design Science Discipline

Chapter 2 discussed the theoretical background of the Design Science discipline. Section 3.1 deals with the development of Design Science in the sense of frameworks that give guidance for the execution of design processes and design research cycles. This section introduces the three most cited papers in IS literature and brings their approaches from the perspective of developing a theoretical background. This paper applies the features and point of views of the philosophical underpinning developed in Section 2.3 to analyze whether the discussed frameworks constitute IS research in this special manner. This section gives also an idea of an answer to research question 3 by preparing the underlying fundament of each framework. The use of the core subject matter of each framework will be regarded in connection with research question 2 and finalized in chapter 4.

3.1   Three Different Design Science Frameworks

Design Science has become an important area of IS research that builds up a bridge between theory and practice. Prototypes and implementations are essential elements for solving practical issues confronted by business units. Design Scientists are able to study the relevance of the systems they build in an organizational context. However, not many IS researchers are able to focus on prototyping or the Design Science approach because they do not have the necessary skills (Au 2001). Design Science is a prescriptive discipline that requires a conceptual framework to guide researchers and practitioners through the process of conducting, evaluating, and presenting Design Science (Hevner et al. 2004).

This paper introduces the frameworks suggested by Walls et al. (1992), March and Smith (1995), and Hevner et al. (2004), as they are the three papers most often cited in Design Science history (March and Storey 2008). In addition to the number of citations in other academic literature, these papers have also been chosen because of their (unintentional) connection points among each other and their being taken together being able to provide a complete foundation for a Design Science research cycle (Vahidov 2006). Three steps can be identified in the research cycle, with each step described by one framework. Walls et al. (1992) have introduced the concept of (1) theories of design. March and Smith (1995) defined the (2) research outputs of Design Science. Hevner et al. (2004) provided (3) guidelines for conducting Design Science research (Vahidov 2006).

A brief introduction of each framework is provided in the next section, with a special focus on the separation of Design Science and the Natural Sciences, the use of theory, and the paradigmatic background of each framework. Furthermore, this paper tries to give an idea, how each framework has contributed to the development of Design Science. The definition of the core subject matter of the frameworks is beyond the scope of Chapter 3, but is analyzed more deeply in Chapter 4.

3.1.1 Building an Information System Design Theory for Vigilant EIS

Walls et al. (1992) are some of the earliest authors[1] to articulate the need for a class of theories to be incorporated into the design process of IS research. Their concept was the first to try to set up a class of theories, which focused on the design process itself (inner environment), instead of trying to find a theory for Design Science as a part of IS research (inner and outer environment) (Carlsson 2006). However, their theory approach is broader than just the construction of an artifact, as they state that the beginning of the design process is defined by problem identification (Venable 2006). The authors argue that Design Science is in need of a set of theories that are not borrowed from reference disciplines with a view to strengthening the discipline and the design process at its core. The motivation to develop special design theories is explained by the prescriptive nature of design. The theories that can be borrowed from the Natural Sciences are not able to define goals that need to be reached through a process. Design theory sets up these goals and, furthermore, gives guidance as to how to reach it. *"IS design theories make the design process more tractable for developers by focusing their attention and restricting their options, thereby improving development outcomes. In addition, IS design theories inform researchers by suggesting testable research hypotheses"* (Markus et al. 2002, p. 180).

One special characteristic is the usefulness for practitioners. Design theories such as those of Walls et al. (1992) propose the methods that are required to reach a goal. Although the authors want to set up theories for the special design process in IS research, they recognize that the design theories need to involve some theories from Natural Sciences, as the elements of the design process are subject to natural laws. A

---

[1] Nunamaker et al. (1991) already described the need for Theory Building as a strategy of their multimethodological approach to IS research.

design theory needs *"to be a prescriptive theory which integrates normative and descriptive theories into design paths intended to produce more effective information systems"* (Walls et al. 1992, p.36).

As this paper noted before, Weber (1987) argued that the designed artifact is also a subject to natural laws. This is partly true, but again Walls et al. (1992) showed that the natural laws and the theories of the Natural Sciences are not able to fully deal with a Design Science concept. A special set of design theories is needed. Walls et al. (1992) are therefore not separating Design Science from Natural or Behavioral Science; they are combining necessary elements from the Natural Sciences with the basic understanding of a design process. These design theories are not losing sight of the realistic construction of real world phenomena.

Design Product		
1.	Meta-requirements	Describes the classes of goals to which the theory applies.
2.	Meta-design	Describes a class of artifacts hypothesized to meet the meta-requirements.
3.	Kernel theories	Theories from natural or social science governing design requirements.
4.	Testable design product hypotheses	Used to test whether the meta-design satisfies the meta-requirements.
Design Process		
1.	Design method	A description of procedure(s) for artifact construction.
2.	Kernel theories	Theories from natural or social sciences governing design process itself.
3.	Testable design process hypotheses	Used to verify whether the design method results in an artifact, which is consistent with the meta-design.

Table 2: Components of Information System Design Theory (Walls et al. 1992)

Walls et al. (1992) pick up the idea introduced by Simon (1969), which defines that design is a process to change a present situation into a preferred one (i.e. the fulfillment of a goal) and that a product is needed as proof-of-concept of the underlying theory. They continue to use this concept and integrate it into their definition of design being a product and a process. These two aspects need to be reflected by a design theory, as the headlines in Table 2 show.

The components of the IS design theories, seen in table 2, are not explained in detail in this paper. Instead it should be stressed that the authors differentiate between an artifact that can be implemented to solve a single problem and a class of artifacts that are the elements, which design theories focus on. Design Science is an area of research that deals with classes of problems rather than just applying available knowledge to solve a special problem. Walls et al. (1992) also realize the importance of generating new knowledge by introducing meta-requirements, meta-design, and kernel theories (see Table 2) that are effective for a whole class of goals, artifacts, and theories. The design product is constrained by natural or social laws. Kernel theories display these constraints, which are also valid for the whole class of requirements posed to the design product. The design process is subject to similar requirements and constraints. The design process and the product hypotheses determine whether the meta-design applied satisfies the meta-requirements, i.e. whether the designed artifact is consistent with the meta-design applied.

According to Walls et al. (1992) IS design theories need to be subject of testing. Their procedure for testing is value driven. The designed element is tested in context of an IS and compared to the value of an alternative system. The implementation of the artifact is necessary, as the theory is only able to provide an answer, if the meta-design/design method satisfies the meta-requirements/meta-design rather than answering, if the design element achieves a relevant outcome in the business environment. The value testing method is based on empirical validation. The applied mathematical models and proofs indicate that the authors are acting upon the Positivist paradigm. Goals are defined and designed elements seek to achieve these goals through the use of technology. However, the reality is knowable with probability (see Table 1) and the designed artifact is not able to change the social context. The knowledge, which is generated and controlled through the design theories, is obtained through quantitative methods.

Object of analysis	Characteristic
Separation of Design and Natural Science	Integrated approach: Kernel theories adopted from natural laws embedded in IS design theories.
The use of theory	Development of IS design theories.
Paradigmatic background	Positivist paradigm. Evaluation with quantitative methods.

Table 3: The Use of Essential Elements in the Framework by Walls et al. (1992)

3.1.2 Design and Natural Science Research on Information Technology

Within the potential Design Science research cycle described in the introduction of this chapter, the framework suggested by March and Smith (1995) provides the second stage towards completing the picture. Walls et al. (1992) pointed out the importance of an IS design theory. March and Smith (1995) take the lead in developing the next step in this fictional research cycle. Even though the authors did not reference Walls et al (1992), they are on the same track following Simon's (1969) call to focus on the design area in IS research. The authors realized that organizational problems and tasks occur in relation with the practical use of IT, which are not adequately represented in the constructions, implementations, and evaluation criteria. Human requirements need to be represented in the real world; IT can be an instrument *"developed in response to specific task requirements using practical reasoning and experiential knowledge"* (March and Smith 1995).

In their introduction, March and Smith (1995) immediately make the point that IT research is a subject of the Natural Sciences and Design Science. IT systems can be built and studied; furthermore, an IT system is implemented within a context that is already described by the Natural Sciences or will be subject of research in one of the traditional disciplines. The authors attempt to clarify how both approaches are different in their core orientation. The descriptive Natural Sciences "theorize" and "justify", whereas the prescriptive Design Science "builds" and "evaluates". However, the separating line that has been drawn between Natural Science and Design Science in this introduction is not impervious. March and Smith (1995) do not consequently separate or combine the both science approaches; maybe they are on the horns of a dilemma to support the claim of Design Science to be a serious field of research with a different research objective on the one hand, but they have recognized that IS research and Design Science, on the other hand, cannot be regarded independently. They state that possible difficulties in Design Science arise from the environment of the artifact and its influences that are studied by the Natural Sciences; at the same time they remark that the interactions between both areas of research are appreciated.

It should not be criticized that March and Smith (1995) demonstrate the relatedness of the research disciplines, which is based on Simon's (1969) specification of the inner and outer environment of a design artifact. However, the connection is not strong enough to fix the perception of Design Science being a discipline of applied knowledge (practice), instead of being a pure research discipline that is able to produce new knowledge (Weber 1987). Without quoting Walls et al. (1992), the authors introduce the same thought concerning natural laws constraining the artifact that is otherwise described as kernel theories. This framework does not include the natural law boarder in an integrated approach of Design Science and the Natural Sciences because "*notably absent from this list [of Design Science products] are theories, the ultimate products of natural science research*" (March and Smith 1995, p.253-254). The absence of theory and theorizing in this framework can indirectly be identified by the statement that Design Science should construct an artifact for a specific purpose and evaluate its utility. In contrast to this opinion, Walls et al. (1992) tried to establish an understanding that Design Science needs to address a whole class of yet unsolved problems. This will give Design Science the status of a pure discipline with the ability to be relevant for practical use.

The specifications of the Natural Sciences are still important for the Design Science framework in this paper. The characteristics that theorize and justify are set in parallel with the design characteristics build and evaluate. All four activities are included in the research framework as arranged by March and Smith (1995).

Research Activities

		Build	Evaluate	Theorize	Justify
Research Outputs	Constructs				
	Model				
	Method				
	Instantiation				

Figure 4: Design Science Research Framework (March and Smith 1995)

Figure 4 represents the Design Science research framework proposed by March and Smith (1995). It can easily be seen that the x-axis of the framework-matrix is constructed by all four characteristics disposed from both science areas. Natural Sciences are still important for gathering insights into the functionality of IT artifacts. As we did in the analysis of the previous paper, the special parts of the framework will not mentioned in detail. However, the building blocks of this framework are helpful to show the separation of Design Science, the use of theory and the paradigmatic background.

First of all the paper puts the Design Science characteristics "build" and "evaluate" on the same level as mentioned by Walls et al. (1992). Artifacts are constructed to solve a problem with a feasible solution. The evaluation process is value based and conducted with advice from a reference system. The difference between each solution can be quantitatively measured. The evaluation process gives an answer as to whether the designed artifact delivers a more effective outcome. This is described as progress in IS research. March and Smith (1995) describe that the evaluation process only determines "how well" an artifact works and not "how" or "why" it works.

Again, a clear boarder between applied science and pure science is missing. It is not excluded that the more effective artifact is build upon already available knowledge taken out of the knowledge base of a reference discipline. It is not necessarily said that the IS field requires new knowledge to realize practical progress. Without evaluating how or why an artifact could possibly solve a problem, a Design Scientist can apply the knowledge prepared by Natural Scientist. Therefore, design would not be considered serious IS research.

The Natural Science characteristics are furthermore needed to identify why a constructed artifact works effectively within the given environment. In contrast to Walls et al. (1992), March and Smith (1995) do not indicate which special requirements highlight these goals. Instead, building an artifact is the first step of the research activities and theorizing is put at the back of the research cycle. Given this ordering, design scientists are not able to identify real world phenomena and problems that are existent within organizations, as the Behavioral Science approach has not been incorporated in this first step. It seems as if the problem space is set randomly or not existent at all. The paper by March and Storey (2008) diminishes this impression by referring back to Simon's (1969) position. This paper describes that a major challenge for the IS discipline is describing, *"desired organizational information processing capabilities and their relationship with present and desired organizational situations (...)"* (March and Storey 2008, p.726). However, they still have not yet incorporated this approach into their framework, leaving the identification of these capabilities to other disciplines.

Theory is needed to clarify how the artifact works and how the interaction with the environment is achieved. In terms of Simon (1969) this would count as a design theory because this theory examines why the present situation changed into a preferred one. It observes the space between the inner and outer environment, and the conception of the inner environment, and the interaction of the design process at both "boarders". The last step of justifying the design theory is a proof, if the explanation given by theory is valid or not. March and Smith (1995) want to give a scientific answer instead of just noticing that the designed artifact is solving the required tasks.

The main contribution of this framework to the Design Science knowledge base is the conceptualization of the research outputs. Up to this point the framework displays an interlinking of two scientific areas with present research instruments. The different research outputs presented on the horizontal axis in Figure 4 are components of the design process. The framework distinguishes between:

- Constructs – special language and knowledge of the discipline

- Models – description of problem through the use of constructs

- Methods – algorithms or guidelines that form the frame of the problem set

- Instantiations – Implemented computer-based system within an organization

(March and Storey 2008)

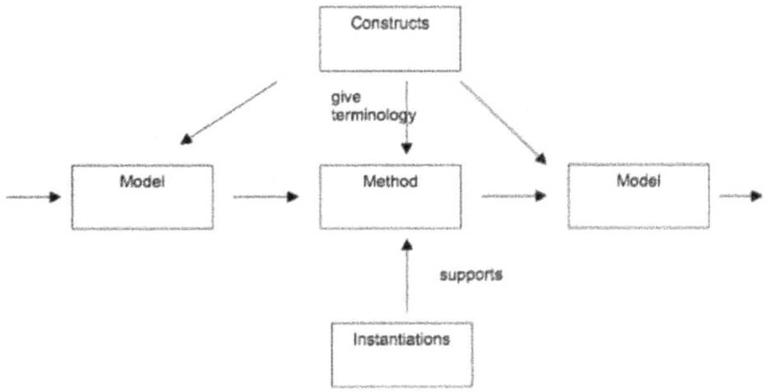

Figure 5: Relation between Research Outputs (own Diagram following March and Smith (1995))

Related by Walls et al. (1992), this framework distinguishes between a design product (implementation) and a design process (methods, models) that leads to the final product. However, the design process is composed of elements that can be subject to evaluation, theorizing, and justification themselves. Constructs, models, and methods can exist without being part of a final instantiation. Figure 5 depicts the relationship between the elements of the design process. Models and methods are constrained and influenced by the terminology and conceptualizations of the defined constructs. The constructs are the regulation framework that assures the consistent procedure within each design process. Models can be used to set up the problem space, which is needed to set up the guidelines and to construct the artifact. At the same time they represent the problem assembled with the methods. The instantiation is the proof-of-concept of the method applied and demonstrates the feasibility of the developed artifact.

In strong connection with the Natural Science influences, March and Smith (1995) act on the basis of the Positivist paradigm. Based on the utility and statistical decision theories introduced by Simon (1969), the authors rely on quantitative methods to build and evaluate IT artifacts (March and Storey 2008). Separated from the influences of the Natural Sciences, the design process in this framework is not going to change the social context at all. It is not up to Design Science to identify the needs and capabilities of the organizational framework of the artifact. March and Smith (1995) concentrate on technology serving the requirements of the social world.

Object of analysis	Characteristic
Separation of Design and Natural Science	Research activities on basis of Natural and Design Science. Design Science is influenced by Natural Science but acts independently in constructing the IT artifact.
The use of theory	Theory building is outside the scope of Design Science. Natural Science theory is needed to discover how and why an artifact works.
Paradigmatic background	Positivist paradigm. Construction and evaluation with quantitative methods.

Table 4: The Use of Essential Elements in the Framework by March and Smith (1995)

3.1.3 Design Science in Information System Research

After a decade without considerable articles promoting the Design Science discipline, the paper by Hevner et al. (2004) was widely accepted and quoted in IS Design Science (Venable 2006). In the Design Science research cycle, depicted in this paper, the framework by Hevner et al. (2004) builds the last step towards its completion. The authors introduce seven guidelines for conducting efficient and effective design research. They mention both frameworks analyzed before and use some of their suggestions to set up a valid framework. Reading the paper, it soon becomes clear that the separate consideration of Behavioral Science (part of the Natural Sciences) and Design Science is adopted from March and Smith (1995). Furthermore, the authors describe both research approaches as paradigms of IS research. IS Behavioral Science research is seen as the traditional way of predicting and explaining the impact of instantiations in the system, made up of people, organizations, and technology. March and Smith (1995) mentioned four research activities. Likewise this paper uses the design characteristics "creation" and "evaluation" as a second part of the IS research cycle. According to March and Smith (1995), this framework does not distinguish consequently between each paradigm. *"Truth and utility are two sides of the same coin and (...) scientific research should be evaluated in light of its practical implications"* (Hevner et al. 2004, p. 77). The characteristics of Behavioral Science, most notably the understanding of organizational problems, are not incorporated into a Design Science approach.

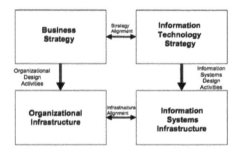

Figure 6: Organizational Design and Information System Design Activities (Hevner et al. 2004)

In contrast to March and Smith (1995) the authors understand that a problem space is needed. However, they distinguish between the broader approach of IS research (including organizational design) and the focused domain of Design Science (information system design) shown in Figure 6. Both design activities need to be undertaken separately, with the focus of IS design being on building the IS infrastructure within the business context. The approaches exist with similar importance and are based on different strategies (see Figure 6). Although both strategies are oriented towards each other, they are not integrated within one approach. This point of view strengthens the importance of Design Science utilizing the technological instruments. It is not yet clear how this IS cycle can produce artifacts with a relevant outcome.

Based on the design characteristics "build" and "evaluate", the idea of design being a process and a product is adopted from Walls et al. (1992) to set up a build-and-evaluate loop to finalize the design artifact through reassessing the feasibility. Hevner et al. (2004) use the design products and design processes formalized by Mach and Smith (2005) to generate their framework without diverging from their basic orientation.

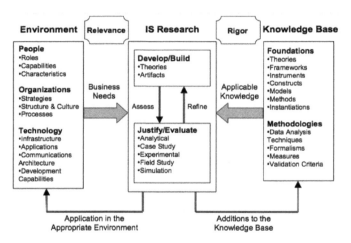

Figure 7: Information System Research Framework (Hevner et al. 2004)

Figure 7 presents the complete framework, which is valid for IS research, instead of just focusing on the design factors. IS research is framed by the environment and the knowledge base. The environment sets up the problem space for a relevant phenomenon, which is mainly defined by Behavioral Science aspects. This is the same with the knowledge base. Theories taken out of reference discipline, in equal measure with design results from earlier research efforts, are the foundations of relevant IS research. However, Design Science addresses unsolved problems in innovative ways, and is not about implementing existing knowledge. The knowledge base provides the instruments to undertake the research process.

The IS research, as core of the framework, is set up differently compared to March and Smith (1995). The characteristics of Behavioral Science and Design Science are compared in each stage of building an artifact. Instead of dividing "develop" and "build", these merged elements form the artifact that is applied in the appropriate element. The outcomes of the combination "develop" and "justify" represent the additions to the knowledge base. However, Hevner et al. (2004) are not defining the IT artifact as a combined approach of Behavioral Science and Design Science, this is only subject of IS research instead of designing. The importance of this restriction is outlined in Chapter 4.

Hevner et al. (2004) provide seven guidelines to support researchers, reviewers, editors, and readers in understanding and conducting effective Design Science research. Each of the guidelines need to be addressed to conduct complete Design Science research. The guidelines are outlined in Table 5 but are not examined in detail in this paper.

Design as an Artifact	Constructs, models, methods, and instantiations need to be produced in Design Science research.
Problem Relevance	Important and relevant business problems provide the objective of Design Science research.
Design Evaluation	Evaluation methods need to quantify the utility, efficacy, and quality of an artifact.
Research Contributions	Research contributions must be made in the area of design artifact, foundations, and methodologies.
Research Rigor	Rigorous methods in construction and evaluation need to be applied to constitute Design Science research
Design as a Search Process	An effective artifact is subject to a search process to reach a desired end.
Communication of Research	The outcome of Design Science research must be presented to design scientists, as well as to users without technological knowledge.

Table 5: Design Science Research Guidelines (own Table following Hevner et al. (2004)

By introducing the two paradigms Behavioral Science and Design Science, Hevner et al. (2004) attempt to strengthen the approach of Design Science in IS research. Besides mentioning a Design Science paradigm, they are not building something like Socio-technologist approach that would be different than existing paradigms. The evaluation process in their paper is quantitatively driven. The Behavioral Science impact and interplay with Design Science is descriptive and not able to change the social world. Design Science must give answers to present problems without changing the environmental context. These attributes are based on the Positivist paradigm with a slight impact of the interpretive point of view. People, technologies and organizations are seen separately. People are able to influence the social setting and are one component to be regarded for a relevant outcome of IS research.

Object of analysis	Characteristic
Separation of Design and Natural Science	IS research is based on of Behavioral Science and Design Science. Design Science is the core discipline without Behavioral Science influence.
The use of theory	Theory is subject of the Natural Sciences. Theories are needed to develop the basis for IT artifacts. Design Science is affected by these theories.
Paradigmatic background	Behavioral Science and Design Science are named paradigms. The quantitative approach points out the use of the Positivist paradigm with slight influences from the interpretive approach.

Table 6: The Use of Essential Elements in the Framework by Hevner et al. (2004)

4 Identifying the Core Subject Matter of Design Science in IS research

The previous chapters have examined the development of Design Science in IS research, the question of a theoretical background, and the characteristics of selected Design Science frameworks. This paper already made clear that a Socio-technologist paradigm is favored by the author in connection with influences from the Positivist and Interpretive paradigm. However, the main research question (2) has not been considered thus far: What is the core subject matter of Design Science in IS research? Before analyzing different core subjects of Design Science and its approaches, it should be clarified as to why the focus on a core subject is so essential for IS research, and why this focus could possibly solve the discipline's current identity crisis.

This paper follows the opinion of Becker et al. (2007) that the identity crisis of IS or is emerging out of three major conflicts. The first conflict is headlined as "rigor vs. relevance". Some scholars argue that rigorous research methods, combined to those used in the Natural Sciences, are not able to produce relevant outputs that deal with the phenomena posed by organizations. Without forming a problem space and implementing an artifact an effective and efficient outcome cannot be realized. The answer to this criticism is two-sided. Relevant design often lacks rigorous research methods. The contribution made by practitioners does not necessarily generate sufficient knowledge, which could be part of the Design Science knowledge base. The "applied" design process does not qualify as a research discipline. Based on this first conflict, the second dispute deals with the question as to whether Design Science is an independent discipline. The implementation of an artifact requires information from the Behavioral Science discipline to deal with the claims made by people, organizations, and technology already in use. This incorporation of other disciplines leads to the allegation that Design Science does not have an own identity and is not able to support the core subject of IS research. The conflict, if Design Science should only be technology oriented, instead of employing Behavioral Science elements, is strongly connected with this question.

All three conflicts are justified because IS research has not yet identified a core subject matter for Design Science, which incorporates the ideas and requirements of all scholars, practitioners, and users. The following sections discuss two approaches for defining a core subject. Section 4.1 summarizes the beliefs that the IT artifact should be the core subject matter of IS research and Design Science respectively. Section 4.2 argues that the work system replaces the IT artifact as core subject of Design Science in IS research because without incorporating the environment no relevant output can be generated.

4.1 The IT Artifact

The frameworks by Hevner et al. (2004) and March and Smith (1995) exclude the Behavioral Science influences from the design process of an IT artifact. The core process of building the artifact is regarded as the main contribution to IS research.

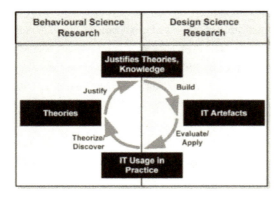

Figure 8: Information System Research Cycle (Becker et al. 2007)

Behavioral Science and Design Science both are components of the IS research cycle, as shown in Figure 8. However, the authors mentioned thus far state that they mainly focus on technology design (Hevner et al. 2004). Chapter 3 highlighted that Behavioral Science and Natural Science are needed to theorize and justify the IT artifact (March and Smith 1995; Hevner et al. 2004) but building and evaluating the artifact is only subject to Design Science research (see Figure 8).

The paper most often cited in connection with the use of the IT artifact is by Orlikowski and Iacono (2001). Their call to theorizing the IT artifact is an important review of articles published in Information Systems Research over the past decade. Although they want researcher to focus more intensively on the IT artifact, their work does not separate Behavioral Science and Design Science as consequently as do the frameworks by March and Smith (1995) and Hevner et al. (2004). Their call to theorizing the IT artifact is based on the belief that the researchers of the IS discipline have turned away from their core subject matter. This lack of attention is their major concern. *"The opportunity (to engage with the IT artifact) arises because the diversity of IS research uniquely qualifies our field to pay special attention to the multiple social, psychological, economic, historical, and computational aspects of (...) technologies (...)"* (Orlikowski and Iacono 2001; p. 130). IT artifacts have cultural and computational capabilities and are embedded in a social environment. However, the reader should not mix up the understanding of IS research and Design Science. As Figure 8 shows, the IS research cycle naturally incorporates Behavioral Science (March and Smith 1995; Hevner et al. 2004), but Design Science as one part of IS research and is not trying to integrate the social influences on basis of a Socio-technologist paradigm. The theorizing of specific technologies (Orlikowski and Iacono 2001) is their indirect focus that can be applied to Design Science.

A more drastic view of the core concept is given by Weber (2003). He argues that the IS discipline needs an identity, which is completely isolated from reference disciplines. In his earlier paper (Weber 1987) he pointed to the difference between an applied research and a pure research discipline. This idea has been formalized into an identity concept on basis of distinct theories, which are completely novel and "unused" by other disciplines. Regarding the social influence on IS research, Weber (2003) argues, that *"if we conclude that psychological theories can be used or readily adapted to account for user performance with different types of human-computer interfaces, however, we will have done little to contribute to the core of information system discipline"* (p. vi). The newly developed theory must be untouchable by other disciplines in order to contribute to the core of IS. Weber (2003) tries to develop the theory out of information system-related phenomena. Explicitly, he excludes theories that describe the interaction of technology and humans. He concludes with the identification of designed representations as the core of the IS research. He is not using the expression "IT artifact"; however, he is describing that the design process of representations (implementations) is the core. This drastic separation of Behavioral Science and Design Science goes along with his call for a pure IS research discipline (Weber 1987).

Another paper addresses the concerns of Orlikowski and Iacono (2001) and Weber (2003). This paper is by Benbasat and Zmud (2003), who try to find a way to articulate the core properties of IS research in a narrower way than Weber (2003). First of all they introduced the concept of Exclusion Errors that can be connected with the Orlikowski and Iacono (2001) paper. In their opinion a lot of IS research was conducted without focusing on the IT artifact at all. IS researchers mainly focused on behavioral concepts and forgot about their underlying discipline.

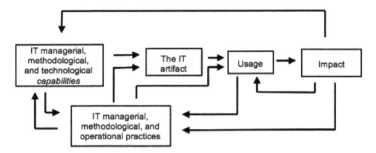

Figure 9: IT Artifact and Its Immediate Nomological Net (Benbasat and Zmud 2003)

Figure 9 shows the 'nomological net', which implies the necessary elements to conduct relevant IT research. The IT artifact is set as the core of the research cycle. Benbasat and Zmud (2003) incorporate the impact of the IT artifact but only up to the point where it is essentially connected with the understanding of the artifact. The IS core needs to be identified from among the special opportunities of the discipline. The nomological net incorporates abilities, which are integral parts of IS. The influences of reference discipline need to be damped.

On the other side Benbasat and Zmud (2003) mention the concept of Errors of Inclusion, which goes along with the call from Weber (2003). Inclusion appears, *"when IS research models involve the examination of constructs best left to scholars in other disciplines"* (Benbasat and Zmud 2003, p.190). Constructs are the language of a discipline (March and Smith 1995) and this language needs to be free of the impact of reference disciplines.

The question, whether the IT artifact is the core subject matter of IS research cannot yet been answered due to the different approaches of frameworks guiding through Design Science. However, as an answer to research question 3 the development shows that IS scholars use the special focus on the Design Science in connection with the IT artifact as its core (most recently Hevner et al. 2004). This discipline is gaining influence through these justifications. Although the most cited papers rely on the approach depicted in Figure 8, the practical value of incorporating Behavioral

Science elements into IS research is supported by some scholars (e.g. Alter 2003). The next section opposes the approach by analyzing why IT work systems should be the core subject matter of the IS field. By presenting a second possible approach to clarify the core subject matter, it should be clear that the discipline is still in search for a single definition. The IT artifact shaped up as the "naturally" build core subject matter that was formed over time and has not yet reached its final definition. The conflict between relevant outputs and rigorous research comes up again at this point. Researchers use the IS environment they need to present their special work. Some authors try to support the work system in order to incorporate more influences into the discipline.

4.2   The IT Work System

This paper has set the foundation for a system as the core subject matter rather than the IT artifact by recommending the Socio-technologist paradigm as philosophical underpinning for Design Science. Chapter 2 mentioned that the 3 paradigms could ideally be combined in a mutimethodological approach (Gregg et al. 2001; Nunamaker et al. 1991). This approach cannot be the basis for an IT artifact being the core subject matter of IS research. However, this paper also mentioned in Chapter 3 and Section 4.1 that this conception is widely used. One paper by Alter (2003) answers this approach with the call for the IT work system being the core subject matter of the IS field. In recognition of the widely used approach analyzed in Section 4.1, this paper will only give a brief insight into the conceptualization of the work system by Alter (2003). An evaluation of both approaches and an estimation of the further use of this concept are given in the conclusion and outlook of Chapter 5.

The work system framework (Figure 10) gives an idea why the IT artifact cannot be regarded as the core subject matter within this approach. A work system is subject to many impacts given by strategies, infrastructure, and environment. The system identifies several sub-systems, many of them belonging to the Natural Sciences, but also technological sub-systems. Becker et al. (2007) *"emphasize that focusing on the relevant system – the social and technical sub-system – is a necessary precondition for conducting relevant research"* (p. 128). The work system approach is much more practical orientated, focusing on the phenomenon of interest. This field of research outlines itself from the Positivist and Interpretive paradigms. The work system research cycle is able to identify, render, analyze, and finally change a phenomenon of interest (Becker et al. 2007). This changing impact is out of reach for the Positivist paradigm frameworks.

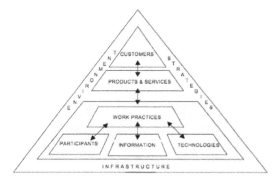

Figure 10: The Work System Framework (Alter 2003)

Without being able to incorporate Behavioral Science characteristics, IS is only able to produce artifacts. This production is in need of theory and knowledge; again the discipline obtains an applied character, which is undesirable (Weber 1987).

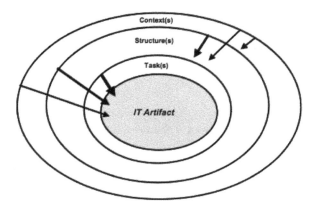

Figure 11: Possible Focus Areas in IS Research (adopted from Benbasat and Zmud 2003)

Finally, figure 11 displays the possible focus areas of IS research. The IT artifact is a central concern, but it is strongly enclosed by the systems causing its existence.

5   Conclusion and Outlook

The Design Science discipline is in the spotlight of IS research. Practitioners and users of technical systems are calling for special IT artifacts that treat the upcoming organizational problems in an efficient and effective way. To focus on this new way of solving problems the IS researchers have developed a design discipline by incorporating elements out of reference areas such as engineering, architecture, and the industry. Designing artifacts requires a revised understanding of the IS discipline being an area of research. Identifying and solving problems are centered in this new approach but the need for theory and theorizing is identified. The IS researchers must define a broad fundament for the new discipline by formulating new concepts to deal with this normative methodology.

Instead of explaining the existent world new ideas of creating useful and implementable knowledge are required. Although this approach is somehow opposed to the traditional sciences, only their influences can form the whole picture. Artifacts are constrained by natural laws and the social system. Real world phenomena are subject to the interaction of people, organizations, and already available IT systems with an explanation given by available and new created theories. By cutting this environment away, Design Scientists make the mistake of forgetting about the natural development of Design Science. Without an unobstructed implementation of the artifact the research will be useless for the audience asking for solutions. The implementation shows that the artifact realizes the desired outcome that is only necessary within the social context. This paper has shown that the separation of Natural Sciences and Design Sciences leads in the wrong direction. Rigorous research can be conducted on basis of the Socio-technologist paradigm in connection with the available paradigms. By focusing only on the technological side of IS research the reference disciplines will overtake the important role of foreseeing and explaining the interaction of newly developed artifacts and the organization and IS research is left with the adaption of available knowledge. This conclusion is limited by the continuing search of the core subject matter of the IS discipline. Scholars have focused on the IT artifact, because they are able to explain and expand this field without borrowing from other disciplines. Some scholars want to establish a "pure" discipline by isolating from all outer influences. The historic development has shown that this wish will not come true. Modern organizations cannot be seen in pieces that are not connected with each other at all. The interplay of the single business units within the organizational context is the main area in need for new answers. The IT work system displays such an approach addicted to the Natural Sciences. However, both think tanks need to be unified to tightening an important and assertive Design Science discipline in IS research. The matters of the Design Science frameworks have shown that problems out of the real business world need to be solved efficiently and effectively. Probably the scholars themselves have created the identity crisis, but it makes the discipline stronger because they have recognized their increasing importance. A lot of papers have focused the identity of Design Science. With a stronger focus on conducting high quality Design Science research, a discussion about the underlying concept is maybe not needed.

This paper mainly mentioned the problems faced by Design Science and the IS discipline. A final answer for defining a core subject matter cannot be given due to the different approaches analyzed before. Each author faces challenges of making his work relevant in a special environmental setting. Further research needs to focus on the possible merge of the different Design Science approaches and their contact with other science disciplines. Furthermore, frameworks need to be connected or compared to extract the useful elements that have proven relevance. A research area focusing the practical impact must incorporate all partners that benefit from the designed artifact. Further research should specify the social setting and the role of each member within this context. Design Science will play a major role in the future even without a strong theoretical foundation.

References

- Alter, S. (2003). 18 Reasons why IT-reliant Work Systems should replace "The IT Artifact" as the Core Subject Matter of the IS Field, Communications of the AIS, Vol. 12, pp. 366-395

- Becker, J.; Niehaves, B. and Janiesch, C. (2007). Socio-Technical Perspectives on Design Science in IS Research, Advances in Information Systems Development, pp. 127-138

- Benbasat, I. and Zmud, R. (1999). Empirical Research in Information Systems: The Practice of Relevance, MIS-Quarterly, Vol. 23, No. 1, pp. 3-16

- Benbasat, I. and Zmud, W. (2003). The Identity Crisis within the IS Discipline: Defining and Communicating the Discipline's Core Properties, MIS-Quarterly, Vol. 27, No. 2, pp. 183-194

- Carlsson, S. (2006). Towards an Information System Design Research Framework: A Critical Realist Perspective, DESRIST 2006, pp. 192-212

- Grant, D. (1979). Design Methodology and Design Methods, Design Methods and Theories, 13, No. 1

- Gregg, D.; Kulkarni, U. and Vinzé, A. (2001). Understanding the Philosophical Underpinnings of Software Engineering Research in Information Systems, Information Systems Frontiers 3:2, pp. 169-18

- Gregor, S. (2002). Design Theory in Information Systems, Australian Journal of Information Systems, Vol. 10, No. 1, pp. 14-22

- Gregor, S. (2006). The Nature of Theory in Information Systems, MIS-Quarterly, Vol. 30, No. 3, pp. 611-642

- Hevner, A. and March, S. (2003). The Information System Research Cycle, IT System Perspective, November 2003, pp. 111-113

- Hevner, A.; March, S.; Park, J. and Ram, S. (2004). Design Science in Information Systems Research, MIS-Quarterly, Vol. 28, No. 1, pp. 75-105

- Kuechler, B.; Vaishnavi, V. and Kuechler, W. (2007). Design Science Research in IS: A Work in Progress, http://home.aisnet.org/displaycommon.cfm?an=1&subarticlenbr=386#ISDR history

- March, S. and Smith, G. (1995). Design and natural science research on information technology, Decision Support Systems 15, pp. 251-266

- March, S. and Storey, V. (2008). Design Science in Information Systems Discipline: An Introduction to the special Issue on Design Science Research, MIS-Quarterly, Vol. 32, No. 4, pp. 725-730

- McKay, J. and Marshall, P. (2005). A Review of Design Science in Information Systems, Sixteenth Australasian Conference on Information System, pp. 1-11

- Newell, A. and Simon, H. A. (1976). Computer Science as Empirical Inquiry: Symbols and Search, Communications of the ACM, Vol. 19, No. 3, pp. 113-126

- Nunamaker, J.; Chen, M. and Purdin, T. (1991). Systems Development in Information System Research, Journal of Management Information Systems, Vol. 7, No. 3, pp. 89-106

- Orlikowski, W. and Baroudi, J. (1991). Studying Information Technology in Organizations: Research Approaches and Assumptions, Information System Research, 2:1, pp. 1-28

- Orlikowski, W. and Iacono, C. (2001). Desperately Seeking the "IT" in IT Research-A Call to Theorizing the IT Artifact, Information Systems Research, Vol. 12, No. 2, pp. 121-134

- Owen, C. (1997). Design Research Building the Knowledge Base, Journal of the Japanese Society for the Science of Design, Special issue, 5 No. 2, pp. 36-45

- Peffers, K. and Tuunanen, T. (2006). The Design Science Research Process: A Model for Producing and Presenting Information System Research, DESRIST 2006, pp. 84-106

- Pries-Heje, J. and Baskerville, R. (2008). The Design Theory Nexus, MIS-Quarterly, Vol. 32, No. 4, pp. 731-755

- Purao, S. (2002). Design Research in the Technology of Informations Systems: Truth or Dare, GSU Department of CIS Working Paper. Atlanta

- Srinivasan, A.; March, S. and Saunders, C. (2005). Information Technology and Organizational Contexts: Orienting our Work along Key Dimensions, Twenty-Sixth International Conference on Information Systems, pp. 991-1001

- Vahidov, R. (2006). Design Researcher's IS Artifact: A Representational Framework, DESRIST 2006, pp.19-33

- Venable, J. (2006). The Role of Theory and Theorising in Design Science Research, DESRIST 2006, pp. 1-18

- Walls, J.; Widmeyer, G. and El Sawy, O. (1992). Building an Information System Design Theory for Vigilant EIS, ?, pp. 36-59

- Weber, R. (1987). Toward a Theory of Artifacts: A Paradigmatic Base for Information Systems Research, Journal of Information Systems, 1:2, pp. 3-19

- Weber, R. (2003). Still Desperately Seeking the IT Artifact, MIS-Quarterly, Vol. 27, No. 2, pp. iii-xi